EMOTIONAL INTELLIGENCE skills assessment

EISA

Participant Workbook

Steven J. Stein
Derek Mann
Peter Papadogiannis
Wendy Gordon

Pfeiffer
A Wiley Imprint
www.pfeiffer.com

MHS
Emotional Intelligence
Assessments and Solutions

Acquiring Editor: Holly J. Allen
Marketing Manager: Tolu Babalola
Director of Development: Kathleen Dolan Davies
Developmental Editor: Susan Rachmeler
Editorial Assistant: Dani Scoville

Production Editor: Michael Kay
Editor: Rebecca Taff
Manufacturing Supervisor: Becky Morgan
Composition: Classic Typography
Design: Adrian Morgan and Gearbox

Printed in the United States of America

Printing 10 9 8 7 6 5 4 3 2

Contents

Workshop   1

Part I.   Introduction and Overview   3
Part II.   What Is Emotional Intelligence and Why Is It Important at Work?   7
Part III.   The Five Factors of Emotional Intelligence   15
Part IV.   Perceiving   25
Part V.   Managing   31
Part VI.   Decision Making   39
Part VII.   Achieving   47
Part VIII.   Influencing   53
Part IX.   Understanding Your Results   57
Part X.   Developing Your Emotional and Social Skills   67

Development Exercises   75

Perceiving   76
Managing   91
Decision Making   97
Achieving   103
Influencing   121

Development Strategies   131

Perceiving   132
Managing   133
Decision Making   134
Achieving   135
Influencing   136

Resources and Endnotes   137

Workshop

Part I. Introduction and Overview

The purpose of this workbook is two-fold:

1. During the Workshop

The information in this workbook will help you better understand how emotional and social skills impact performance, and what you can do to strengthen your effectiveness by using these skills appropriately.

2. For Ongoing Development

After the workshop, you can use this workbook as a resource for ongoing individual development to increase your emotional and social functioning. You will apply these concepts and principles to improve your own and your group's performance. Exercises are divided into five main areas designed specifically to address issues encompassing your intra- and interpersonal behaviors. Completing these exercises will make you more aware of how important emotions are in your daily decision-making, problem-solving, and stress-tolerance abilities. Additionally, there is a strategies section that provides suggested steps you can take to improve in each of the five areas.

How do people in the workplace generally see emotions? Are you seeing a shift in the belief that emotions should be "checked at the door" when coming to work?

"I view emotions as organizing processes that enable individuals to think and behave adaptively."

Peter Salovey, Ph.D.,
Yale University's Department of Psychology, prominent researcher in the field of emotional intelligence

If yes, what do you think has created that shift?

DID YOU KNOW?

- The term "emotional and social intelligence" refers to the skills that people use to manage their own emotions wisely, i.e., use emotions to help them achieve their goals and to manage their interactions with others in ways that maximize the chances of influencing others constructively.

What are some ways emotions have been seen as dangerous distractions to be minimized and controlled?

- Emotions, when used correctly, can make us smarter than intellect alone.
- Research shows that emotions used wisely make us more effective in the workplace. Emotional intelligence research has shown it to be positively related to teamwork behavior,[1] job performance,[2] and leadership.[3]

Based on the traditional definitions of EI, Mann and Papadogiannis[4] have proposed a new definition that places emphasis on the social component of emotional intelligence:

> "Emotional and social intelligence is the ability to accurately assess, interpret, manage, and express emotions and solve problems of a personal and interpersonal nature toward realizing the pursuit of realistic and meaningful objectives."

Workshop Objectives

1. Discover the major components of emotional intelligence.

2. Recognize the behaviors and characteristics of an emotionally intelligent person.

3. Identify areas in which emotional intelligence skills can be applied.

4. Learn about your own emotional strengths and growth opportunities.

5. Generate action steps you can take to improve your emotional and social abilities and your own success.

Part II.
What Is Emotional Intelligence and Why Is It Important at Work?

Emotion and Performance

Examples of emotion facilitating someone's performance at work:

Examples of emotion impairing someone's performance at work:

DID YOU KNOW?

- The words emotion and motivation come from the same root Latin verb *motere*, which means "to move."

Exercise

Your Competency Model/Values Statement

Which of your competencies/values are primarily emotionally or socially based, as opposed to those based on technical skills alone?

Emotional

Technical

_____ _____

_____ _____

_____ _____

_____ _____

_____ _____

_____ _____

_____ _____

Emotional Intelligence Skills Assessment (EISA)

Anatomy of a Reaction

Do you agree that some emotions are more conducive to getting particular jobs done? If yes, why?

DID YOU KNOW?

- Mild anxiety helps us in analytical tasks, while a sense of safety helps us to be creative.

Imagine that, while we are in this meeting, the fire alarm sounds. What do you feel?

Exercise

The Effects of Mood on Detailed Work

Scenario 1

Instructions: Scan the grid below and circle the numbers in sequence, starting from number 1. You have one minute to work on this task.

3	72	43	28	93
25	46	16	9	39
64	49	53	27	86
89	23	13	34	20
1	48	35	44	14
68	26	51	2	95
45	91	24	65	67
70	63	6	54	33
31	8	88	69	42
10	90	11	66	36
37	52	59	77	73
78	21	99	47	81
100	17	41	74	96
71	32	22	19	98
15	62	29	12	7
40	55	38	80	57
94	75	79	83	61
56	92	84	87	4
85	97	50	76	82
30	18	5	60	58

Scenario 2

Instructions: Scan the grid below and circle the numbers in sequence, starting from number 1. You have one minute to work on this task.

6	69	3	27	31
100	87	54	65	15
63	21	19	94	42
17	85	76	68	12
51	2	35	88	52
9	67	89	5	90
28	91	14	43	74
70	45	80	37	25
84	22	47	26	83
10	95	4	59	34
92	57	29	96	38
32	98	82	71	61
40	7	48	56	8
79	75	30	23	81
66	53	50	16	73
58	11	78	49	33
72	97	39	44	62
46	55	60	41	93
36	64	13	77	20
24	18	86	99	1

Four-Step Process

Step One: An emotion comes up.

Record how you feel right now.

Step Two: Emotions affect our thinking by directing our attention.

Record the thoughts that your feelings directed you to.

Step Three: Ask insight questions.

What is causing these feelings?

Where are your feelings coming from?

Step Four: Action step.

How do you want to feel at the end of the day today?

What do you need to do to achieve the feelings that you want?

Part III.
The Five Factors of Emotional Intelligence

The EISA provides an assessment of emotional intelligence (EI) along five core factors, which can be developed to maximize emotional and social functioning. These five factors are illustrated in the model below and are described in more detail on the next few pages.

Perceiving
The ability to accurately recognize, attend to, and understand emotion.

Decision Making
The appropriate application of emotion to manage change and solve problems.

Achieving
The ability to generate the necessary emotions to self-motivate in the pursuit of realistic and meaningful objectives.

Influencing
The ability to recognize, manage, and evoke emotion within oneself and others to promote change.

Managing
The ability to effectively manage, control, and express emotions.

Perceiving
Definition: The ability to accurately recognize, attend to, and understand emotion.

This EISA factor measures your ability to:

- Understand your own emotions
- Stay attuned to the emotions of others
- Demonstrate empathy
- Differentiate between emotions

The ability to perceive emotions starts with being aware of emotional signals, accurately identifying what they mean, and then applying them to a given situation. The better someone is at reading and understanding emotions, the more appropriately that person will be able to respond.

LOW	HIGH
Those who are less skilled at Perceiving	**Those who are very skilled at Perceiving**
• Have difficulty discriminating between emotions	• Discriminate between emotions
• Exhibit less positive emotion	• Gauge intensity of feelings
• May be emotionally unpredictable	• Are empathic
	• Tend to be emotionally predictable

How might this factor influence your work?

Managing
Definition: The ability to effectively manage, control, and express emotions.

This EISA factor measures your ability to:

- Effectively manage emotions
- Effectively control emotion
- Appropriately express emotions

The ability to manage one's emotional experience is perhaps the most important factor of emotional intelligence for social interaction. Emotions generally arise from the appraisal of our environment and our interpretation of it. Being able to manage our emotions and the emotions of others alters the level and intensity of the emotion both experienced and expressed. For example, if you are overly anxious each time your boss asks you to come into his or her office, you might misinterpret the message he or she is trying to convey to you.

LOW	HIGH
Those who are less skilled at Managing emotions	Those who are very skilled at Managing emotions
• Mismatch emotions	• Show appropriate expressions
• Cope less effectively with stress	• Have enhanced coping skills
• Have difficulty building rapport and emotional networks	• Have more meaningful interpersonal relationships

How might this factor influence your work?

Decision Making

Definition: The appropriate application of emotion to manage change and solve problems.

This EISA factor measures your ability to:

- Use positive emotions
- Use negative emotions
- Manage change and emotions to solve problems

Your mood is highly influential in judgments and decision making. The process of decision making requires the attention to and processing of relevant environmental, intra- and interpersonal cues. An emotionally intelligent individual is well equipped to recognize the need to engage specific emotions to facilitate the decision-making process. Positive and negative emotions (i.e., happy versus sad) directly influence the resources (both mental and physical) that are allocated to the decision process required for task completion. For example, at times, positive emotions such as happiness, elation, and exuberance tend to be associated with an overestimation of the likelihood for positive outcomes and an underestimation of the probability for a negative outcome. A mismatch of mood and context may impact the chances of making the appropriate decision.

LOW	HIGH
Those who are less skilled at Decision Making tend to	Those who are very skilled at Decision Making are
• Generate emotions that are less appropriate for the task at hand	• Able to generate an emotion that is most appropriate for the task at hand
• Be impulsive or paralyzed	• Flexible
• Make untimely decisions	• Pragmatic
• Make inaccurate decisions	• Perceptive

How might this factor influence your work?

Achieving

Definition: The ability to generate the necessary emotions to self-motivate in the pursuit of realistic and meaningful objectives.

This EISA factor measures your ability to:

- Self-motivate
- Generate requisite emotions
- Realize the pursuit of realistic and meaningful objectives

Motivation has been linked with satisfaction, enjoyment, and interest in life. Individuals with lower motivation tend to have a difficult time adjusting to change and may be more prone to burnout. As a result, those individuals who are driven to achieve tasks and possess confidence in their ability to achieve report better mood and adjustment. For example, people who use their emotions to achieve their goals are often motivated to succeed and spend less emotional energy and time thinking about failure. This intrinsic motivation results in the experience of positive emotions that often result in increased optimism and self-confidence.

"Go-Getters" vs. People in a Rut

How are these people different? How do you feel when you're with them?

LOW	HIGH
Those who are less skilled at Achieving	Those who are very skilled at Achieving
• Avoid risk	• Are intrinsically motivated
• Are outcome-oriented	• Take pleasure in success
• Avoid emotions associated with failure	• Take responsibility
• Have little task ownership	• Tend to be in a good mood
	• Enjoy moderate risk

How might this factor influence your work?

Influencing
Definition: The ability to recognize, manage, and evoke emotion within oneself and others to promote change.

This EISA factor measures your ability to:

- Appraise a situation
- Interpret emotional tone
- Evoke emotions
- Promote change

Emotions play an enormous role in the creation and maintenance of social relationships. A person's verbal tone, the words expressed, facial features, and body language are all factors that can shape the behaviors, thoughts, and emotions of others. Inferences made by others based on emotional information can influence power, competence, and credibility. An individual's ability to evoke emotions in others may inspire others to achieve greater goals, influence their creativity, and improve collaboration.

LOW	HIGH
Those who are less skilled at Influencing	Those who are very skilled at Influencing
• Are rarely assertive or ineffectively assertive	• Are effectively assertive
• Prefer one-on-one communication	• Have a confident demeanor
• Have difficulty managing others	• Are optimistic
• Tend to be instructive	• Inspire others

How might this factor influence your work?

Exercise

Famous People Brainstorming

My group's EISA factor: _____

Famous people (real or fictional) who exemplify this EISA factor:

How do these people perform this skill successfully?

(List your observations beside each name.)

(Optional) Famous people (real or fictional) who do not use this factor well:

How do you know these people don't perform this skill well?

(List your observations beside each name.)

Note Taking

Part IV. Perceiving

Exercise

Perceiving and Interpreting Scenarios

This activity is designed to provide you with an opportunity to develop the skill of identifying and interpreting emotions.

With a partner or in a small group, using one of the following scenarios (your facilitator will tell you which one), your objective is to identify what emotions need to be perceived and expressed by you in order for you to have a successful outcome. Each scenario is designed to provide you with a contextual framework. Read through the scenario and record your thoughts.

Scenario 1: The Clock Is Ticking

You have been with your current organization for many years and have managed to develop many great relationships with your colleagues. Mary is a co-worker whom you have known for less than a year; she works across the hall from you. Late Monday morning, while you are in the middle of a pressing deadline, Mary knocks on your door and asks if she can come in to talk. Mary is a dependable employee, but is rather quiet and removed from your social network at work. Mary indicates that she has some personal news to tell you.

What emotions do you believe need to be perceived and expressed in order to make Mary feel supported by you?

My Own Emotions

Perceived	Expressed

Scenario 2: Collaboration

The president of your organization has established a committee of top performers who are responsible for establishing the mission of the department for the next five years and has appointed you as committee chair. Your committee consists of three project managers, two account coordinators, and one administrator. Your goal is to have your mission statement and action steps to achieve the mission in place at the end of three months.

Your committee started by meeting once per week, with plenty of energy and vigor. Everyone was excited about the possibilities and opportunities that the project presented. However, just a month and a half into the project, the meetings have deteriorated and productivity has come to a halt. Committee members often argue among themselves about job responsibilities, priorities, decision making, and even the relationships that are forming within the group.

What emotions do you feel need to be perceived and expressed in order to motivate the committee to achieve the goals that were set?

My Own Emotions

Perceived	Expressed

Scenario 3: Feedback

You are a consultant who was hired to conduct an analysis of job applicants for a senior executive position. You have used various assessment tools and techniques for building your case for and against the prospective applicants. Unexpectedly, the president of the organization has asked you to deliver the feedback to the leading candidate that he will not be promoted.

What emotions do you feel need to be perceived and expressed in order to give proper feedback to the candidate?

My Own Emotions

Perceived	Expressed

Note Taking

Part V.
Managing

>> Managing a Reaction

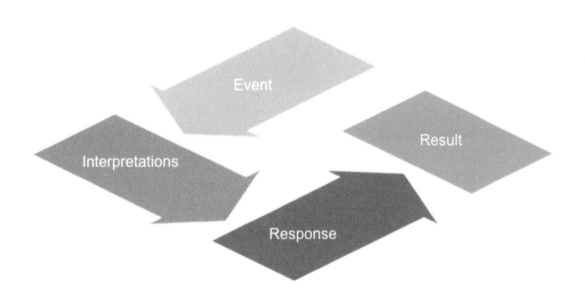

Emotion Log

The objective of this exercise is to bring about a conscious awareness of the emotions that you experience on a regular basis and the impact these emotions have on your daily functioning.

Your ability to change and sustain change requires an astute awareness of how you feel, think, and act. This exercise will help you develop a deeper understanding of how your emotions are affecting you and those you interact with.

You'll do Step 1 of this exercise in the workshop and Steps 2 and 3 on your own after the workshop.

Step 1: Awareness

From the list of emotions presented below, circle a minimum of ten emotions that most accurately represent what you experience throughout a typical day. If you circle more than ten emotions, that is perfectly fine.

dynamic	energetic	vigorous	relaxed	comfortable	easy	calm
merry	happy	confident	certain	sure	delighted	overjoyed
resolute	excited	thrilled	brave	bold	daring	dashing
inspired	motivated	stimulated	lighthearted	carefree	nice	pleasant
fast	alert	afraid	fearful	scared	panicky	angry
irritated	distressed	anxious	apprehensive	worried	concerned	alarmed
depressed	doubtful	uncertain	indecisive	worn out	helpless	unsafe
intense	fierce	jittery	nervous	uneasy	restless	sorry
tense	strained	tight	rigid	tired	weary	exhausted
determined	pleased	quick	furious	dissatisfied	inactive	regretful
set	satisfied	rapid	violent	discouraged	sluggish	sad
exhilarated	glad	agreeable	aggressive	disturbed	insecure	unhappy
peaceful	quiet	unhurried	cheerless	lazy	dispirited	annoyed
rapid	contented	settled	cheerful	active	morose	frustrated

Step 2: Record and Log

In the space provided, record the ten emotions you experience most on a day-to-day basis as identified from the list on the previous page. Cut out the card and make ten copies. For the next ten days, you are to rate the utility and intensity of the emotions you have experienced. *Utility* refers to the effect of the emotion. For example, was the emotion helpful or harmful to the situation? *Intensity* refers to the severity of the emotion experienced (0 = no feeling; 10 = maximum intensity).

Emotion	Intensity	Utility (Helpful or Harmful?)
1. _____	0 1 2 3 4 5 6 7 8 9 10	_____
2. _____	0 1 2 3 4 5 6 7 8 9 10	_____
3. _____	0 1 2 3 4 5 6 7 8 9 10	_____
4. _____	0 1 2 3 4 5 6 7 8 9 10	_____
5. _____	0 1 2 3 4 5 6 7 8 9 10	_____
6. _____	0 1 2 3 4 5 6 7 8 9 10	_____
7. _____	0 1 2 3 4 5 6 7 8 9 10	_____
8. _____	0 1 2 3 4 5 6 7 8 9 10	_____
9. _____	0 1 2 3 4 5 6 7 8 9 10	_____
10. _____	0 1 2 3 4 5 6 7 8 9 10	_____

Cut out ✄

Step 3: Reflection

After each day, think about the different emotions that you have experienced. Compare those emotions with the emotions that you experienced on other days. Are there emotions that you are experiencing more often than others? If yes, please be aware of what they are. If the intensity of those emotions is high (8 to 10), try to understand what is triggering these emotions and how they may be harmful to your performance at work.

The ABCs of Emotions

This exercise will enable you to better understand your emotional beliefs and subsequent actions, while better preparing you for more positive action.

One of the reasons people have trouble managing their emotions is that their belief systems often get in the way of their ability to think and act rationally. For example, imagine getting called into your supervisor's office. What goes through your mind?

>Why am I being called in?

>What have I done wrong?

>What have I done right?

>Uh oh!

Generally, people tend to feel that something bad is going to happen, such as being reprimanded or fired. We often make decisions with little or no information. Reframing our beliefs, however, can improve our ability to understand our environment because we allow ourselves time to challenge and reorganize our irrational beliefs.

For this activity, you'll work through the event described above as a group, but you can also use this process on your own to examine any event.

Activating Event: Identify the event that elicited an emotional reaction from you.

My boss calls me into her office for an impromptu meeting

Belief(s): Identify your beliefs that lead to your emotional reaction.

Something must be wrong. She never does this. A meeting without warning, something is definitely wrong. Did I do something wrong? I don't remember!

Consequences: What were the results of your thoughts and reactions to that event?

Stress, Anxiety, Worry, Apprehension, Uncertainty

Disputing Your Beliefs: Were your initial appraisals of the event accurate? If not, why?

Just because this situation with my boss is new doesn't mean it is going to be bad. There could be so many different reasons why she wants to meet.

Effective Beliefs: How might you have appraised the situation differently?

I just have to go in there with an open mind and deal with it the best that I can. I am very good at what I do and I have a pretty strong relationship with my boss. She does not make decisions hastily. Why would today be any different?

Focus: Identify how you can better manage your emotions.

I can stop for a moment and appraise the situation without jumping to conclusions. I need to just relax, collect my thoughts, and make decisions with the proper emotional perspective.

Note Taking

| Emotional Intelligence Skills Assessment (EISA)

Part VI.
Decision Making

Exercise

Processing Decisions

Your decision-making process, ability, and success are directly influenced by the emotions you experience and how you choose to cope with those emotions. Failing to regulate and/or evoke an appropriate emotion can be catastrophic to performance. The following exercise is designed to guide you through your decision-making process. As you work through this activity, be as descriptive as possible.

Step 1: Problem Identification

Describe a meaningful challenge that you have recently faced.

Step 2: Solution Process

Describe your solution to the problem and the process you engaged in to come to your final decision.

Step 3: Emotion

Describe the emotions you experienced and how your emotions influenced your judgments, decision making, and actions.

Step 4: Outcomes

How effective was your decision? Identify the steps in your decision-making process that you feel were essential to the outcome. What emotions were potentially harmful to the situation?

Step 5: Feel and See Success

Take a moment to re-create in your mind the problem you have identified. As you begin to think about it, feel it! That is, attempt to transform those feelings into emotions, visions, and sensations that you believe would help lead you to success.

The Emotional Roller Coaster

You have five minutes to individually complete Steps 1 through 4. When directed to do so by the facilitator, you will work in small groups to complete Step 5, for which you'll have ten minutes.

Step 1: 10:30 a.m.

You just found out that you and five other members of your workplace won a substantial amount of money in the lottery.

From the list of emotions presented below, circle the emotions that most accurately represent how you feel after hearing the news:

active	dynamic	energetic	vigorous	relaxed	comfortable	easy	calm
cheerful	merry	happy	confident	certain	sure	delighted	overjoyed
settled	resolute	excited	thrilled	brave	bold	daring	dashing
contented	inspired	motivated	stimulated	lighthearted	carefree	nice	pleasant
rapid	fast	alert	afraid	fearful	scared	panicky	angry
annoyed	irritated	distressed	anxious	apprehensive	worried	concerned	alarmed
dispirited	depressed	doubtful	uncertain	indecisive	worn out	helpless	unsafe
lazy	intense	fierce	jittery	nervous	uneasy	restless	sorry
cheerless	tense	strained	tight	rigid	tired	weary	exhausted
unhurried	determined	pleased	quick	furious	dissatisfied	inactive	regretful
quiet	set	satisfied	rapid	violent	discouraged	sluggish	sad
peaceful	exhilarated	glad	agreeable	aggressive	disturbed	insecure	unhappy

What is the intensity of your emotions after hearing the news?

Intensity

(low) 0 1 2 3 4 5 6 7 8 9 10 (high)

Step 2: 10:35 a.m.

A few minutes after learning that you have won the lottery, one of your direct reports, who has been coming to work late every day for several weeks, comes in late once again. She walks right by you on the way to her workstation, and it looks as though she has a smug look on her face. She works in a small group and the other members of her work group have come to you to complain that her tardiness reduces the effectiveness of the entire group.

From the list of emotions presented below, circle the emotions that most accurately represent how you feel after seeing your direct report.

active	dynamic	energetic	vigorous	relaxed	comfortable	easy	calm
cheerful	merry	happy	confident	certain	sure	delighted	overjoyed
settled	resolute	excited	thrilled	brave	bold	daring	dashing
contented	inspired	motivated	stimulated	lighthearted	carefree	nice	pleasant
rapid	fast	alert	afraid	fearful	scared	panicky	angry
annoyed	irritated	distressed	anxious	apprehensive	worried	concerned	alarmed
dispirited	depressed	doubtful	uncertain	indecisive	worn out	helpless	unsafe
lazy	intense	fierce	jittery	nervous	uneasy	restless	sorry
cheerless	tense	strained	tight	rigid	tired	weary	exhausted
unhurried	determined	pleased	quick	furious	dissatisfied	inactive	regretful
quiet	set	satisfied	rapid	violent	discouraged	sluggish	sad
peaceful	exhilarated	glad	agreeable	aggressive	disturbed	insecure	unhappy

What is the intensity of those emotions after seeing her come in late?

Intensity

(low)   0   1   2   3   4   5   6   7   8   9   10   (high)

| **Emotional Intelligence Skills Assessment (EISA)**

Step 3: 10:45 a.m.

When you confront your direct report with the tardiness problem, she breaks down and cries: she has to drop her son off at school but the school gates do not open soon enough for her to get to work on time. She has been unable to find anyone to take her son to school.

From the list of emotions presented below, circle the emotions that most accurately represent how you feel after hearing your direct report's explanation.

active	dynamic	energetic	vigorous	relaxed	comfortable	easy	calm
cheerful	merry	happy	confident	certain	sure	delighted	overjoyed
settled	resolute	excited	thrilled	brave	bold	daring	dashing
contented	inspired	motivated	stimulated	lighthearted	carefree	nice	pleasant
rapid	fast	alert	afraid	fearful	scared	panicky	angry
annoyed	irritated	distressed	anxious	apprehensive	worried	concerned	alarmed
dispirited	depressed	doubtful	uncertain	indecisive	worn out	helpless	unsafe
lazy	intense	fierce	jittery	nervous	uneasy	restless	sorry
cheerless	tense	strained	tight	rigid	tired	weary	exhausted
unhurried	determined	pleased	quick	furious	dissatisfied	inactive	regretful
quiet	set	satisfied	rapid	violent	discouraged	sluggish	sad
peaceful	exhilarated	glad	agreeable	aggressive	disturbed	insecure	unhappy

What is the intensity of those emotions after hearing the news?

Intensity

(low)   0   1   2   3   4   5   6   7   8   9   10   (high)

Step 4: Decision-Making Time

What decision do you make? Put a check mark by your decision.

☐ *Option 1:* Fire her. Chronic lateness to work is a serious offense and cannot be tolerated any longer.

☐ *Option 2:* Just accept things as they are. You don't have anyone else to take over her role and the gap would set the group's performance back.

☐ *Option 3:* Discuss her problem with the rest of her work team. See whether any alternatives can be brainstormed to help with your direct report's issue.

☐ *Option 4:* Delegate the problem to the work team. After all, empowering them with decision-making authority also makes them more accountable. Plus, you now have some extra money from the lottery; you can decide to take some time off.

☐ *Option 5:* Tell the direct report that her lateness will be no longer tolerated and decide with her on some alternatives to reduce her tardiness.

What emotional state were you in after you made your final decision?

active	dynamic	energetic	vigorous	relaxed	comfortable	easy	calm
cheerful	merry	happy	confident	certain	sure	delighted	overjoyed
settled	resolute	excited	thrilled	brave	bold	daring	dashing
contented	inspired	motivated	stimulated	lighthearted	carefree	nice	pleasant
rapid	fast	alert	afraid	fearful	scared	panicky	angry
annoyed	irritated	distressed	anxious	apprehensive	worried	concerned	alarmed
dispirited	depressed	doubtful	uncertain	indecisive	worn out	helpless	unsafe
lazy	intense	fierce	jittery	nervous	uneasy	restless	sorry
cheerless	tense	strained	tight	rigid	tired	weary	exhausted
unhurried	determined	pleased	quick	furious	dissatisfied	inactive	regretful
quiet	set	satisfied	rapid	violent	discouraged	sluggish	sad
peaceful	exhilarated	glad	agreeable	aggressive	disturbed	insecure	unhappy

Do you think this was the right emotional mind frame to be in?   Yes   No

Did any information distort your decision making?

Step 5: Group Analysis

In your small group, brainstorm some additional decision-making options that may help with this problem.

What does your group think is the right decision?

Note Taking

Exercise

Emotional Goal Setting in Groups

Step 1: Brainstorming

Working in your small group, come up with ten ways to address the issue of work/life balance:

1.

2.

3.

4.

5.

6.

7.

8.

9.

10.

Step 2: Debriefing

As a whole group, you'll have ten minutes to discuss the decision-making process you used in your small groups. Be prepared to share examples from your experience so that everyone can learn. You can record comments on each question below.

1. Was this goal perceived as a threat or a challenge by your group?

2. What was the mood of your group?

3. Think about the emotional reactions your group members had to that goal. Were any of these emotions contagious? Did one person set a positive or negative tone?

4. How did these reactions impact the creativity of your problem solving?

Goal Appraisal

Although goal setting is an instrumental step necessary for the achievement of meaningful objectives, the mere process of creating tangible and meaningful goals that require accountability can be emotionally laden, resulting in the activation of and/or withdrawal from the activity.

The purpose of this activity is to create an awareness of your emotional reactions to a chosen goal while ensuring that a positive and optimal mindset has been established around each goal so as to facilitate goal attainment.

You'll begin this exercise by reading the example on the following page about someone who's been passed over for promotion. Add any of your own thoughts or responses to those already provided. The "positive" or "negative" choice refers to the initial reaction to the event or goal. The 0 to 10 rating refers to the intensity of the emotions related to this event or goal.

Example

Goal

Get a promotion

Intensity

(low) 0 1 2 3 4 5 6 7 ⑧ 9 10 (high)

Goal Appraisal

Negative feelings about my boss. Frustration over a co-worker who was just promoted. Doubt that I will be recognized.

Positive Restructuring

Hopeful about new departmental alignment. Enjoy my job and taking on more responsibility. Committed to working hard and have faith that my contribution will be noticed.

Ideal Emotions

Hopeful, inspired, determined, resolved, energetic, excited, motivated, vigorous, confident.

Your Own Goal

For this page, select a goal of your own choosing and complete the form.

Goal

Intensity

(low)   0   1   2   3   4   5   6   7   8   9   10   (high)

Goal Appraisal

Positive Restructuring

Ideal Emotions

Note Taking

Emotional Intelligence Skills Assessment (EISA)

Part VIII.
Influencing

Exercise

Leadership Qualities

The purpose of this activity is to identify the leadership qualities that are instrumental to exceptional leadership.

Begin this activity by completing Steps 1 through 4; be prepared to share your responses with the group. You'll complete Step 5 when directed to do so by the facilitator.

Step 1: Best Boss

Think of five adjectives to describe your "best boss" ever and record them below:

1. _____
2. _____
3. _____
4. _____
5. _____

Step 2: Worst Boss

Think of five adjectives to describe your "worst boss" ever and record them below:

1. _____
2. _____
3. _____
4. _____
5. _____

Step 3: Differences?

Next, compare and contrast the differences in the words that you chose to describe your "best boss" and "worst boss." Pay particular attention to the differences between the emotional and social skills and technical skills. Write down what trends you see.

Step 4: Behavioral Differences?

In the space provided, list your own behavioral differences (actions, motivations, goals, etc.) while working under your two superiors described above. How did your superiors' demeanor and leadership styles influence your behavior?

Best Boss	Worst Boss

Step 5: Growth

Identify five changes that you would need to make in order to achieve the status of a best boss. Be specific and identify strategies for change.

1.

2.

3.

4.

5.

Note Taking

What the EISA Scores Mean

The scores used in your results graphs are *standard* scores. A standard score takes your raw score (which is simply the sum of your responses) and adjusts it onto a standardized scale to give you more information about what your score actually means and allow you to compare your scores between factors.

Standard scores incorporate the average and the spread of the data around the average (called the standard deviation) into their calculation, resulting in a more informative score. Standard scores for the EISA will always:

- range between 1 and 10
- have an average of 5
- have a standard deviation of 1

This means you automatically know whether your score is above or below average (i.e., above or below 5) and how far away it is from the average (i.e., how many standard deviations of 1 your score is away from 5).

Look at your results graph in your assessment or report. Take some time now to write down your first impressions of your results. Are there any surprises? Do you think your results are accurate?

Note Taking

If you did not take the 360 version of the EISA, please skip ahead to Part X. Developing Your Emotional and Social Skills on page 67.

EISA: 360 Questions to Ask Yourself

Consensus between you and your observers provides confirmation that your self-perceptions about your performance are likely accurate. Generally, job performance tends to be higher when your and your observers' ratings are high and in agreement.

In reviewing your EISA: 360 results, focus on four questions:

1. Are there score differences between you and your observers?

2. Are your observers' scores much higher than your own?

3. Are your scores much higher than those of your observers?

4. Is there a major score difference between your observer groups?

For each question, the facilitator will provide an explanation and an example. Then you'll have time to respond to each question based on your own scores.

1. Are there score differences between you and your observers?

A "score difference" means 1 point or more difference. So in the sample provided, there is not a significant difference between the self score (9.20) and the direct report score (9.34). There is, however, a significant difference between the self score and the manager score (4.86).

Sample: Differences Between Self and Observers

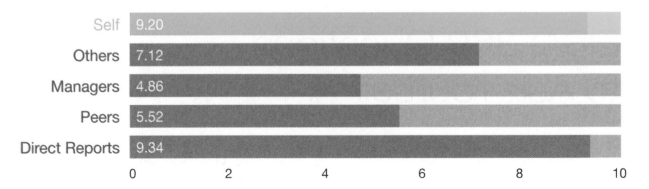

[Perceiving]

Self	9.20
Others	7.12
Managers	4.86
Peers	5.52
Direct Reports	9.34

Now look at your own factor graphs. Are there significant score differences between you and your observers?

If yes, record the factor names and whether your score was higher or lower than the observers' score.

When significant score differences between you and your observers appear, a problem with awareness and consistency may exist. Pay special attention to these areas, because it means your observers see you differently than you see yourself. Think of examples of times you thought you were utilizing the EISA factor in question, and ask yourself why your observers might have interpreted your actions so differently than you did. Questions 2 and 3 will help you direct your efforts further.

2. Are your observers' scores much higher than your own?

There are many plausible explanations for higher scores from your observers in comparison to your own self-perception. One possibility is that you are underestimating your EI ability in some areas. You may have low self-awareness, be holding back, have low self-esteem, hold high self-standards, or you could be overly critical of your performance at times.

Alternatively, you may be experiencing some issues outside of work that may be impacting your score and, in certain situations, you may not be able to summon the emotional strength necessary to function. Because certain observer groups do not have many opportunities to observe you in everyday work activities, they may not be able to give as accurate a depiction of your behavior as you can.

In the sample provided, all observer groups rated the participant higher on the Perceiving factor than the participant rated him- or herself.

Sample: Higher Observer Scores

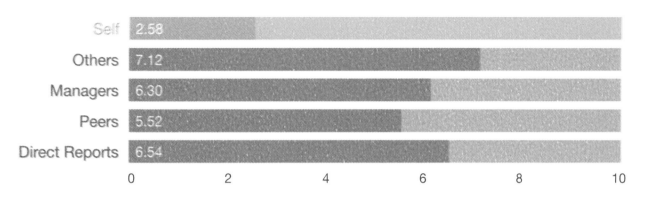

[Perceiving]

Self	2.58
Others	7.12
Managers	6.30
Peers	5.52
Direct Reports	6.54

Now look at your own factor graphs. Are your observers' scores much higher than your own?

If yes, record the factor names and how you account for the difference.

As a follow-up, you can talk to someone you trust (co-worker, family member, friend, executive coach) about your results and consider why there are such variances in the scores.

3. Are your scores much higher than your observers' scores?

Some people overestimate their skills in certain areas when compared to their observers. Sometimes, a higher score indicates a difficulty seeing yourself critically. In order to maintain self-esteem, individuals may actively select the information that puts them in a favorable light. Therefore, self-knowledge is often formed in just the right way to maintain this positive self-image.

Another possible explanation for a higher self-score is that not all individuals have the opportunity to see you in every situation. They may have a limited vantage point and be able to rate you only on a limited portion of your daily activities.

In the sample provided, the participant rated him- or herself higher than any of the observer groups rated him or her.

Sample: Higher Self-Scores

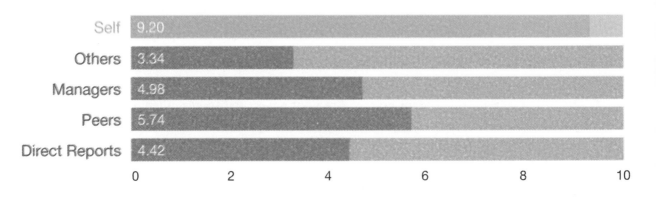

Now look at your own factor graphs. Are your scores much higher than your observers' scores?

If yes, record the factor names and how you account for the difference.

Receiving low results from your co-workers can be surprising and upsetting. When your observers' scores are significantly lower than your own, you may feel skeptical about the value of the assessment or feel angry or defensive. These are all normal reactions. It is not unusual to feel discouraged for being rated lower than expected, or you may have trouble trying to analyze all of the areas that need to be developed. If you find yourself having difficulty moving into a positive, proactive frame of mind, it is important that you take some time to discuss your feelings with the facilitator.

4. Is there a major score difference between your observer groups?

If different groups of observers have diverse scores (for example, your manager scored you high, but your direct reports scored you low), consider the ways you might be behaving inconsistently with different groups. Are you putting on a can-do attitude for your boss, then heaping your worries on your subordinates? Do you feel you can be more open and honest with your peers than with anyone else at work? How might these inconsistencies in your behavior affect the way people see you?

The sample graph shows a variety of observer group scores in relation to the self score.

Sample: Differences Among Observer Groups

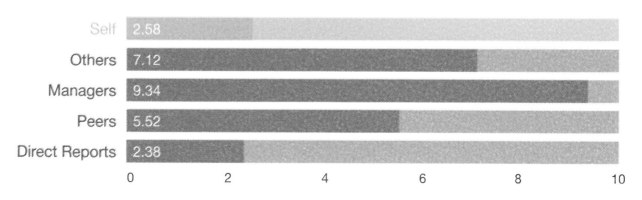

Behaving consistently with direct reports and peers is important to achieving group goals and improving teamwork. In many cases, these two groups spend many hours with you and are in a good position to assess your skills in various settings. A higher score within these groups indicates your ability to motivate others or garner their support when trying to make key decisions and push initiatives forward.

Getting your perceptions in sync with your manager(s) is essential to your overall job success because your manager is in charge of performance evaluations and is the portal to the organization's resources.

If a manager perceives that you have difficulty in handling emotional or social problems, he or she will be less comfortable with your ability to handle technical or interpersonal problems and may hesitate to hand over management issues.

The amount of exposure that you have with different groups also explains variations in perception. Perhaps one observer group has more opportunities to see you using the behavior being rated than another observer group does.

Also, observers can interpret the same behavior very differently. For example, consider a manager who is blunt in his interpersonal interactions. One observer might interpret the behavior as direct, efficient, and precise, while another might see the same behavior as abrupt or even rude. Also keep in mind that an observer's expectations may have an influence on his or her scores.

Now look at your own factor graphs. Is there a major score difference between your observer groups?

If yes, record the factor names, the observer groups, and how you account for the difference.

How might these perceived behavioral inconsistencies cause problems for you at work?

Would you like to change these perceptions about your behavior? If yes, how?

Note Taking

Your EISA Development Plan

Preparing a plan to grow your emotional intelligence (EI) at work is a key step to improving your overall job performance. To improve your EI skills, you must be ready to commit yourself to long-lasting behavioral change. You will not develop these skills for only a few days or weeks; rather, you are committing yourself to developing these skills over the course of your career. Modifying your thoughts and actions is never easy. It takes time, patience, and a lot of practice.

Your Support System

Before embarking on your EI quest, it is important to have a trusted support system in place to help you overcome any obstacles that you may face. This support system will serve as a sounding board for you, where you can discuss what EI skills you are working on and how you are planning to improve these areas. The support system will also help you to stay motivated and focused. By knowing what areas you are working on, the support system can help keep you on track, as well as encouraging you to achieve more. Your support system may include work colleagues, your manager or supervisor, or an executive coach. You might also benefit from resources such as books and training materials.

Below or on a separate sheet of paper, record the names of the people in your support system. Beside each name, indicate how that person will show his or her support.

Once you are fully committed and have your support system in place, continue with the following steps:

1. Identify the EISA areas that you would like to work on or that are most important to success in your current job. If one of your EISA scores is lower, you may want to make that EISA skill a priority.

2. Set goals that are specific to the EISA skill, measurable, and realistic.

3. Identify and address any obstacles that may hinder your goal achievement.

4. Seek out resources that will help you to learn new behaviors. These may include one-on-one coaching, a performance evaluation, or learning from a role model.

5. Continue practicing new behaviors. To improve your job performance, the specific EI skills that you choose to develop need to be repeated, reinforced, and evaluated on a daily basis.

6. Review and reassess your emotional intelligence goals to help solidify what you have learned about emotional intelligence and your job performance. Use the materials on the following pages to help you navigate through your EI journey.

SMARTEST Goal-Setting Plan

Top performers make the time to set clear and realistic goals for themselves and for their teams. Goal setting helps individuals with their focus, persistence, perseverance, and resilience. Reaching one's goals can be accomplished more effectively when goals are **SMART,** that is, they are **S**pecific, **M**easurable, **A**ction-Oriented, **R**ealistic, and **T**imely. Goals that are **E**nergizing, **S**igned, and **T**ested are also critical to improving your job performance.

Use the goal-setting suggestions listed on the next page to help you achieve your EI goals.

Specific—The goals that you set must be specific, without room for generalization. Vague goals are like bad directions; you may eventually get there, but chances are it won't be the most direct or efficient route.

Measurable—Measurable goals are more effective in facilitating long-lasting behavioral change than general "do your best" goals or no goals at all. Ideally, you want to measure your EI goals objectively (with numbers) in order to be able to focus your energy on a specific target.

Action-Oriented—Just saying "I want to do better at my job" doesn't specify what you need to do to accomplish it. You can say all you want, but you must act in order to bring about any real change. Set goals that pertain to specific areas that need to be developed and that are phrased in terms of specific actions you will take in order to turn them into strengths. These kinds of "action goals" help to organize your thoughts, increase persistence, and direct your focus.

Realistic—Set goals that are challenging and ambitious, but that are also achievable. You want to be able to experience success so that you'll be motivated to reach for the next goal.

Timely—When your goals are time-sensitive, they have more motivational impact. Assigning a target date to finish something enables you to better manage and structure your time.

Energizing—Pick an EI goal that is important to your success. If you understand how improving a certain EI skill will improve your overall performance, you will be more motivated to achieve that goal.

Signed—Signing and dating your goals will increase your commitment toward achieving them. By doing this, you will feel more accountable for your actions. Review the terms of your goal-setting plan and make sure that there are no misunderstandings about what will need to be done before signing it. It may also be a good idea to have someone else (such as a supervisor, trusted colleague, or family member) sign your goal-setting plan. This may increase your commitment toward achieving your goals even more.

Tested—Practicing your new beliefs and behaviors is crucial to improving your performance at work. Provide yourself with opportunities to use these new skills in actual situations. Opportunities may include group meetings, interacting with new people at your workplace, or working with difficult co-workers. Accept opportunities to take risks—they might just pay off.

EISA Goal Setting

The steps you take to achieve your performance goals will determine whether or not you succeed in reaching them. To guide your actions, you must create a step-by-step plan.

First, write down the two EISA skills that you want to develop.

1.

2.

List the resources you will need to improve these EISA skills:

List resources you already have that you can leverage to improve these EISA skills:

Now choose the one EISA skill from your list that you want to develop within the next month. Remember to use the **SMARTEST** goal-setting criteria for each goal: specific, measurable, action oriented, realistic, timely, energizing, signed, and tested.

> For example, "I would like to increase my Perceiving skill during four out of five interactions with my direct reports by June 20."

Record this goal on the goal sheet on the next page.

Provide detailed action steps on how you are going to obtain your goal. Each action step should have a specific timeline associated with it.

> For example, "In order to improve my Perceiving skills with my direct reports, I will practice Reflective Listening to confirm my emotional inferences during four out of five interactions by June 12."

You can review the strategy section for your selected skill for ideas and approaches for improving this skill.

Record your action steps on the goal sheet on the next page. In addition to the page you're filling out, there is an additional goal sheet that you can use later when you are ready to develop the second EISA skill from your list.

EISA Goal-Setting Activity Sheet
EISA Goal

Action 1   Deadline: _____ /_____ /_____
                                                                mm   dd   yy

Action 2   Deadline: _____ /_____ /_____
                                                                mm   dd   yy

Action 3   Deadline: _____ /_____ /_____
                                                                mm   dd   yy

Why is this goal important to your success?

What resources can you leverage to achieve your goal?

Signed: _____Date: _____

Witness Signature: _____Date: _____

EISA Goal-Setting Activity Sheet
EISA Goal

Action 1   Deadline: _____ /_____ /_____
                                                          mm   dd   yy

Action 2   Deadline: _____ /_____ /_____
                                                          mm   dd   yy

Action 3   Deadline: _____ /_____ /_____
                                                          mm   dd   yy

Why is this goal important to your success?

What resources can you leverage to achieve your goal?

Signed: _____Date: _____

Witness Signature: _____Date: _____

Note Taking

Development
Exercises

Perceiving

Emotion Profiling

The objective of this exercise is to bring about an awareness of the emotions that are experienced by those around you. Your ability to accurately perceive the tone and intensity of a given interaction enhances your ability to effectively deal with that encounter. From a leadership perspective, the ability to evoke specific emotions and accurately match them to a given situation can go a long way toward earning the respect and appreciation of your group or team. This exercise will help you develop a deeper understanding of the basic human emotions.

Step 1: Vocabulary

It is not uncommon for most people to have a cursory ability to list and describe the basic human emotions. However, in order to accurately perceive, label, and empathize with someone, we must be able to describe and apply our knowledge of the various emotions that can be experienced. Spend time defining each emotion presented below and challenge yourself to identify as many synonyms as you can for each emotion. Record your definition and synonyms of each word in the space provided.

The first one (Anger) has been completed as an example, although you can add your own ideas to those presented.

Anger

Definition: Is an emotional state that may range in intensity from mild annoyance to rage. Anger has physical effects including the raising of one's heart rate and blood pressure and distortion of one's facial features.

Synonyms: irritation, annoyance, fury, ire, outrage, rage, wrath

Disgust

Definition:

Synonyms:

Fear

Definition:

Synonyms:

Joy

Definition:

Synonyms:

Sadness

Definition:

Synonyms:

Surprise

Definition:

Synonyms:

Step 2: Expand Your Thinking

Now it's time to expand your thinking about these emotions. In the space provided, record the many facets of each emotion. Use your vocabulary to paint a picture, detailing the look, sound, and feel of each basic emotion.

For example, in the case of Anger, for "look," you might write "brows pulled down and inward, wrinkles centered above the eyes, eyes opened wide." For "sound," you might write, "stronger intensity, tone, and speed of words." For "feel," you might write, "displeasure or extreme disappointment."

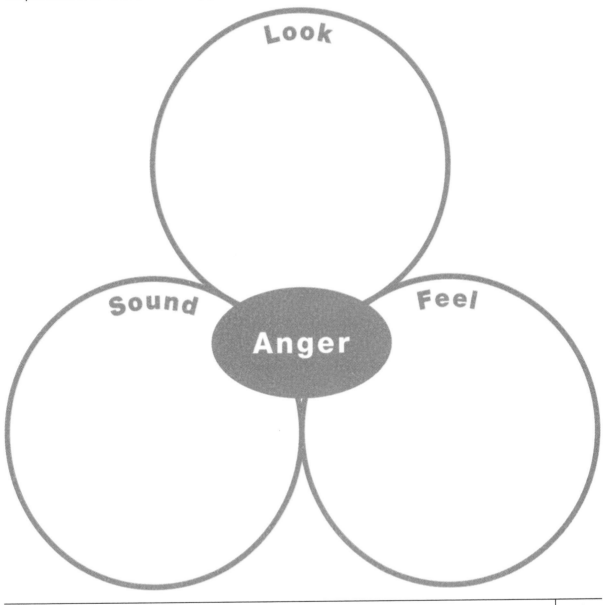

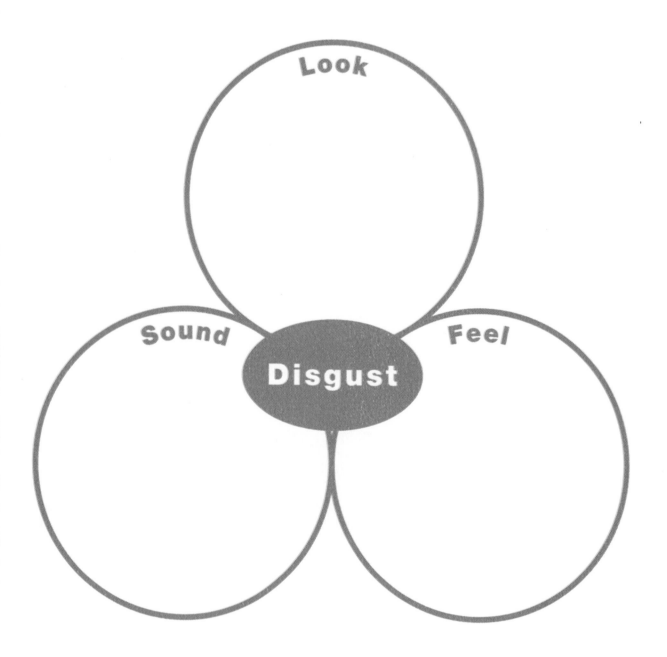

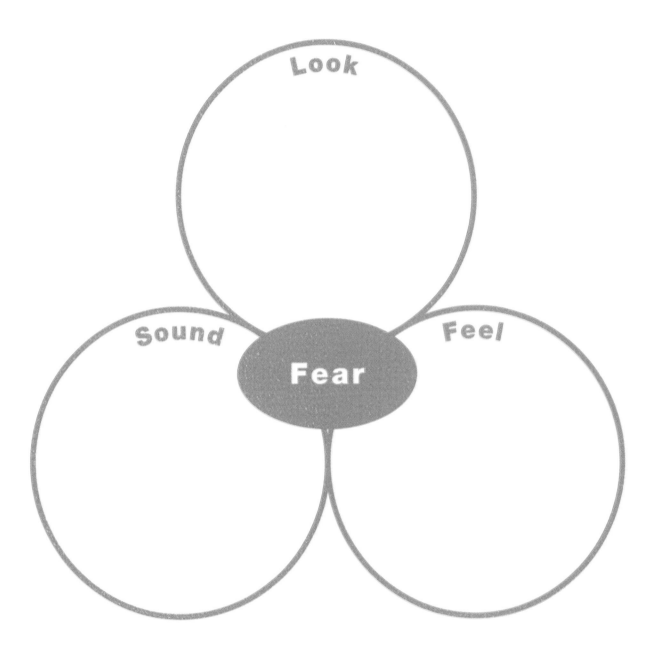

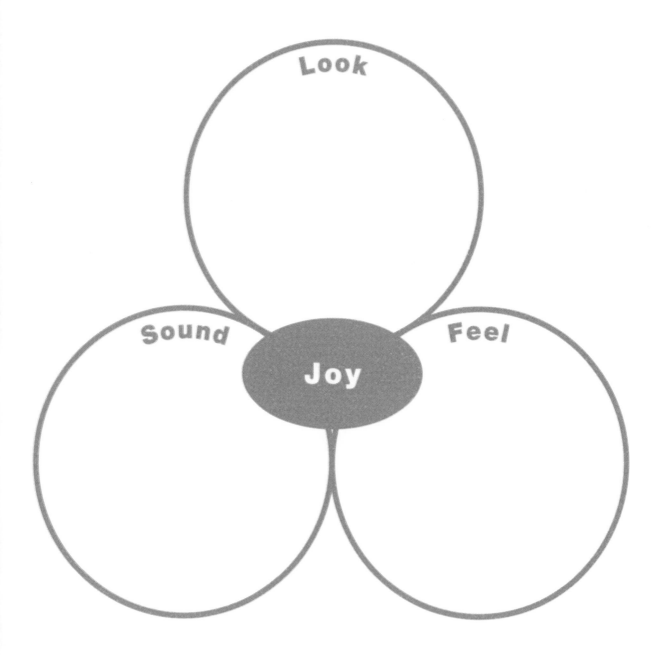

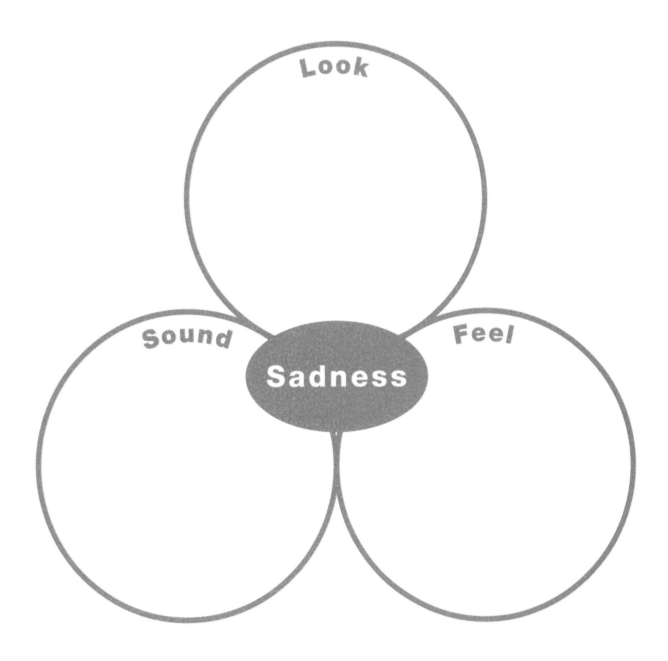

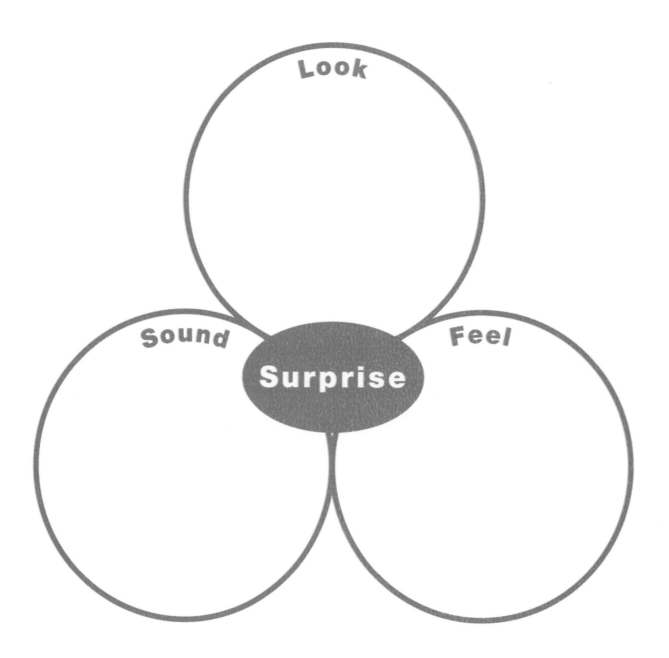

Step 3: Blending Emotions

Consider how many synonyms you were able to list for each basic emotion in Step 1. If you were to return to your list of synonyms and were asked to describe the fundamental difference between these emotions, you would likely identify a difference in the direction (positive or negative) and intensity (low arousal to high arousal) of the emotional experience.

To further your ability to accurately perceive emotions, complete the following blending exercise by solving the emotion equation. Record your answer in the space provided. An answer key is provided on page 86.

Example: Joy + Anticipation = Optimism

1. Anger + Disgust = _____

2. Sadness + Disgust = _____

3. Joy + Acceptance = _____

4. Anticipation + Anger = _____

5. Fear + Anger = _____

Answer Key

1. Anger + Disgust = ___Contempt___

2. Sadness + Disgust = ___Remorse___

3. Joy + Acceptance = ___Love___

4. Anticipation + Anger = ___Aggressiveness___

5. Fear + Anger = ___Jealousy___

Observation Checklist

The objective of this exercise is to further expand your skill set for perceiving an emotional experience. In this exercise you are to simply observe people from a distance. You are not to be involved in or play an active role in the social encounter; you are merely a bystander. You can be creative in the scenarios you observe. For example, observe people interacting in public spaces, at work, on television, or in a movie. Begin practicing alone and then with a friend or colleague, comparing your observations. If discrepancies should occur in your observations, explore possible reasons for the discrepancies.

For each scenario that you observe, complete an observation log. Be sure to attend to the direction (positive or negative) and intensity (0 = low; 10 = high) of the emotion observed. Additionally, in the space provided, identify the emotional trigger that evoked the emotion in the person/people being observed. Then identify the cues that conveyed to you the emotion that was being observed (e.g., body language, tone, facial expressions, etc.). Finally, in the space provided, describe the context in which the identified emotions were observed.

Scene 1:

Emotion Observed	Direction	Intensity	Trigger	Cue
_____	P / N	0 1 2 3 4 5 6 7 8 9 10	_____	_____
_____	P / N	0 1 2 3 4 5 6 7 8 9 10	_____	_____
_____	P / N	0 1 2 3 4 5 6 7 8 9 10	_____	_____
_____	P / N	0 1 2 3 4 5 6 7 8 9 10	_____	_____
_____	P / N	0 1 2 3 4 5 6 7 8 9 10	_____	_____
_____	P / N	0 1 2 3 4 5 6 7 8 9 10	_____	_____
_____	P / N	0 1 2 3 4 5 6 7 8 9 10	_____	_____
_____	P / N	0 1 2 3 4 5 6 7 8 9 10	_____	_____
_____	P / N	0 1 2 3 4 5 6 7 8 9 10	_____	_____
_____	P / N	0 1 2 3 4 5 6 7 8 9 10	_____	_____
_____	P / N	0 1 2 3 4 5 6 7 8 9 10	_____	_____

Scene 2:

Emotion Observed	Direction	Intensity	Trigger	Cue
_____	P / N	0 1 2 3 4 5 6 7 8 9 10	_____	_____
_____	P / N	0 1 2 3 4 5 6 7 8 9 10	_____	_____
_____	P / N	0 1 2 3 4 5 6 7 8 9 10	_____	_____
_____	P / N	0 1 2 3 4 5 6 7 8 9 10	_____	_____
_____	P / N	0 1 2 3 4 5 6 7 8 9 10	_____	_____
_____	P / N	0 1 2 3 4 5 6 7 8 9 10	_____	_____
_____	P / N	0 1 2 3 4 5 6 7 8 9 10	_____	_____
_____	P / N	0 1 2 3 4 5 6 7 8 9 10	_____	_____
_____	P / N	0 1 2 3 4 5 6 7 8 9 10	_____	_____
_____	P / N	0 1 2 3 4 5 6 7 8 9 10	_____	_____
_____	P / N	0 1 2 3 4 5 6 7 8 9 10	_____	_____

Scene 3:

Emotion Observed	Direction	Intensity	Trigger	Cue
_____	P / N	0 1 2 3 4 5 6 7 8 9 10	_____	_____
_____	P / N	0 1 2 3 4 5 6 7 8 9 10	_____	_____
_____	P / N	0 1 2 3 4 5 6 7 8 9 10	_____	_____
_____	P / N	0 1 2 3 4 5 6 7 8 9 10	_____	_____
_____	P / N	0 1 2 3 4 5 6 7 8 9 10	_____	_____
_____	P / N	0 1 2 3 4 5 6 7 8 9 10	_____	_____
_____	P / N	0 1 2 3 4 5 6 7 8 9 10	_____	_____
_____	P / N	0 1 2 3 4 5 6 7 8 9 10	_____	_____
_____	P / N	0 1 2 3 4 5 6 7 8 9 10	_____	_____
_____	P / N	0 1 2 3 4 5 6 7 8 9 10	_____	_____
_____	P / N	0 1 2 3 4 5 6 7 8 9 10	_____	_____

Managing

Body Awareness

The objective of this exercise is to bring about a conscious awareness of the impact your emotional experiences have on your body.

Your ability to change and sustain change requires an awareness of how you feel, think, and act. This exercise will help you develop a deeper understanding of how your emotions make you feel and, in turn, how you appraise those feelings. For example, the manner in which we appraise a situation and the emotions that are experienced can affect our bodies in very different ways. Not being able to cope with stress and anxiety can lead to serious health risks (such as hypertension). If we can recognize what triggers those emotions, our response tendencies, and equip ourselves with adaptive strategies, we can prevent their harmful effects.

Step 1: Record and Log

Cut out the blank card and make seven copies. For the next seven days, you are to identify a series of significant events (events that are meaningful to you) and rate the intensity of your thoughts and feelings as they influence your body (somatic anxiety), level of worry (cognitive anxiety) and your distractibility (wandering mind).

A sample filled-in card has been provided below.

Event	Body	Worry	Distractability
1. Deadlines	0 1 2 3 4 5 6 7 ⑧ 9 10	0 1 2 3 4 5 6 7 8 ⑨ 10	0 1 2 3 4 5 ⑥ 7 8 9 10
2. Performance Review	0 1 2 3 4 5 6 7 ⑧ 9 10	0 1 2 3 4 5 6 7 ⑧ 9 10	0 1 2 3 ④ 5 6 7 8 9 10
3. Team-Building Activity	0 1 ② 3 4 5 6 7 8 9 10	0 1 2 ③ 4 5 6 7 8 9 10	0 ① 2 3 4 5 6 7 8 9 10
4. Doctor's Appointment	0 1 2 3 4 ⑤ 6 7 8 9 10	0 1 2 3 ④ 5 6 7 8 9 10	0 1 2 ③ 4 5 6 7 8 9 10

Cut out ✂

Event	Body	Worry	Distractability
1. _____	0 1 2 3 4 5 6 7 8 9 10	0 1 2 3 4 5 6 7 8 9 10	0 1 2 3 4 5 6 7 8 9 10
2. _____	0 1 2 3 4 5 6 7 8 9 10	0 1 2 3 4 5 6 7 8 9 10	0 1 2 3 4 5 6 7 8 9 10
3. _____	0 1 2 3 4 5 6 7 8 9 10	0 1 2 3 4 5 6 7 8 9 10	0 1 2 3 4 5 6 7 8 9 10
4. _____	0 1 2 3 4 5 6 7 8 9 10	0 1 2 3 4 5 6 7 8 9 10	0 1 2 3 4 5 6 7 8 9 10
5. _____	0 1 2 3 4 5 6 7 8 9 10	0 1 2 3 4 5 6 7 8 9 10	0 1 2 3 4 5 6 7 8 9 10
6. _____	0 1 2 3 4 5 6 7 8 9 10	0 1 2 3 4 5 6 7 8 9 10	0 1 2 3 4 5 6 7 8 9 10

Cut out ✂

Step 2: Take Action

After you have filled out your cards, identify the events that had a high level of intensity, worry, and distractibility. These are the types of events most likely to cause problems at work. The following two activities are designed to help you better cope with this sort of event. These activities are designed to reduce arousal and stress felt within the body while relaxing the mind. When used together, these exercises have been shown to be even more effective. The two activities below will help you in the future when emotional intensity is high.

Progressive Muscle Relaxation

This technique, first described by Edmund Jacobsen,[5] is designed to actively engage the muscles of the body by tensing and relaxing them in a systematic and progressive manner. The key is to sustain a contraction for at least five seconds, but not more than ten, to maximize the number of muscle fibers contracted. This contraction, followed by relaxation, increases the level of relaxation experienced in the muscle. To practice this exercise, do the following:

- Sit comfortably or lie down on the floor with your weight evenly distributed.

- Identify a muscle or segment of your body where you are experiencing tension.

- Contract the muscle with 90 percent effort, followed by relaxing and letting the tension flow out of every muscle.

- Remember to breathe evenly (see below for proper breath control techniques).

Breath Control

We often take breathing for granted and neglect to embrace the natural relaxation properties of proper breathing. For example, when we are relaxed and confident, our breathing is naturally deep and rhythmical. However, when we are stressed or aroused, our breathing becomes shallow and irregular, increasing tension in our mind and body. In a similar fashion to progressive muscle relaxation, when we inhale, muscle tension increases and when we exhale, relaxation ensues. As a result, learning to take a deep, slow, and complete breath can initiate a relaxation response. To effectively implement breath control, do the following:

- Take a slow deep breath that fills the bottom of your lungs first by expanding your diaphragm.

- As you continue to inhale, feel your chest expand, finishing with your chest and shoulders rising slightly.

- Once you have completely inhaled, briefly pause and then slowly exhale, emptying your chest and diaphragm.

- Over time and with practice, you should work toward completing each inhalation in four seconds and each exhalation in eight seconds.

Decision Making

Exercise

Decision-Making Style

The objective of this exercise is to identify your decision-making tendencies and those emotions that can either help or hinder your efficiency and effectiveness. Your decision-making score is reflective of your dominant decision-making style. Your dominant tendencies show when you're under stress or performing in a novel context. However, your ability to remain flexible and adaptable to the context of the problem is equally important when making decisions.

Step 1: Awareness

The first step in this process is to identify three distinct situations in which emotions shaped your approach to making a decision. Describe the context and your decision-making tendency for each situation. Be sure to include a rating of the direction (positive or negative) and intensity (0 = low; 10 = high) of the emotions experienced. An example has been provided.

Example

Had to give a direct report some negative feedback during his performance review. Felt anxious about doing this and afraid that he would take it badly. My anxiety and internal worry about my own performance may have been misinterpreted by my direct report, and further may have distracted me from the situation at hand and made it more difficult for me to perceive and respond to his reactions.

positive / (negative)

| 0 | 1 | 2 | 3 | 4 | 5 | 6 | 7 | (8) | 9 | 10 |

Your Situation Number 1

positive / negative

0   1   2   3   4   5   6   7   8   9   10

Your Situation Number 2

positive / negative

0   1   2   3   4   5   6   7   8   9   10

Your Situation Number 3

positive / negative

0   1   2   3   4   5   6   7   8   9   10

What potential problems does your decision-making style pose for you?

How do you benefit from your decision-making style?

Step 2: Perceiving and Managing the Context

In order for you to enhance your decision-making process, what three changes would you make to your current decision-making style? Be sure to consider what you've already learned about perceiving and managing emotions. How can you implement these changes? When will you implement these changes?

Example

Change: *Feel Less Rushed When Making Decisions*

How to Implement: *Understand the emotions that go into making decisions, what emotions are most important for certain decisions, work on time-management skills.*

By When: *Start immediately and reevaluate in 3 months*

My Changes

1. Change:

   How to Implement:

   By When:

2. Change:

How to Implement:

By When:

3. Change:

How to Implement:

By When:

Achieving

Exercise

Personal Performance Profile

A performance profile is a visual representation of the skills that are essential to achieving your goals. The objective of this exercise is to help you identify critical performance areas, while evaluating your strengths and development needs in these areas, planning for action, and actively evaluating progress in these areas over time.

The first step in this process is to brainstorm what you believe to be the most important skills necessary to excel in your role. As you embark on this first step, write down whatever comes to mind. Do not censor your thoughts or place judgment on these ideas. Record your skills in the space provided, then rank the five most essential skills in order of their importance for your success. Last, transfer the top five skills that you have identified to the performance grid provided and evaluate your current skill level from 1 (low skill) to 10 (high skill) by shading in the designated areas.

Step 1: Brainstorm

In the space provided, identify the skills and traits that you believe contribute to your job performance.

Step 2: Rank

Prioritize your list from above and write your five most critical skills:

1. _____

2. _____

3. _____

4. _____

5. _____

Step 3: Transfer and Evaluate

Plot the top five skills needed to perform your job role successfully on the diagram. Each ring on the graph represents one point ranging from 0 (inner most ring) to 10 (outer most ring). Use this graph to rate your skill level by shading in the appropriate range of rings for each skill. An example has been provided.

Example

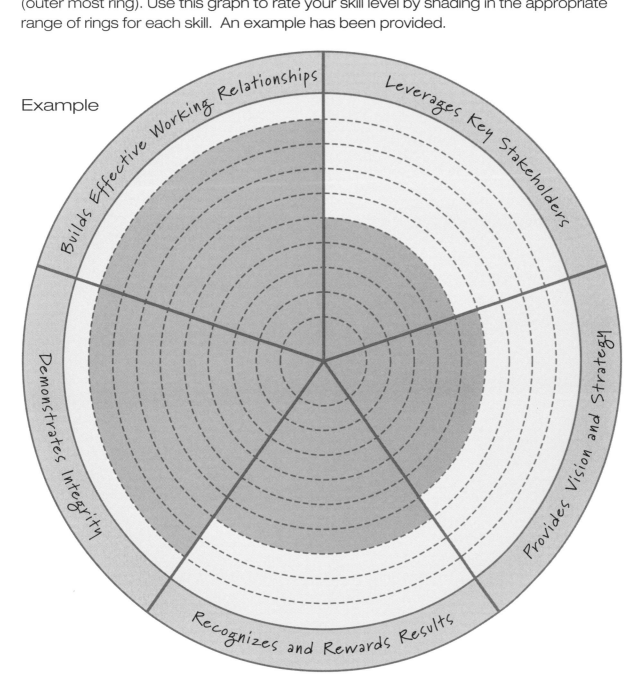

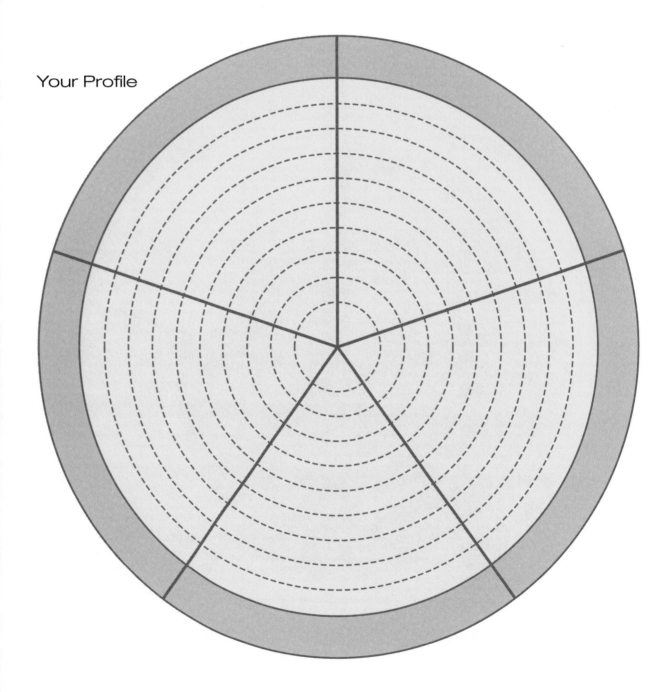

Your Profile

Step 4: Set Your Goals and Re-Assess

At this point you are ready to progress to the Goal-Setting activity (see next exercise). Please consider this a process. That is, as you establish your goals and begin working toward them, continually revisit this Personal Performance Profile activity to monitor and assess the progress you are making along the way. Periodic checks and balances will further assist you in realizing your potential.

Exercise

Goal Setting

Now that you have identified the most important skills necessary to excel in your role, you have set the stage for yourself to set meaningful and measurable goals. This activity is designed to direct your energy toward maximizing your potential.

It is important to consider that goals are statements designed to describe the very objectives you want to achieve; however, they should also include procedural elements to direct your thoughts and actions. Each goal that you establish must be Specific, Measurable, Action-Oriented, Realistic, and Timely. Furthermore, with each goal it is important for you to prioritize its importance and rate its difficulty and intensity.

Step 1: Brainstorm

First, list all the goals that you would like to accomplish in your current job role over the next three months. Remember that this is a brainstorming session, so do not censor your thoughts. Write down whatever comes to mind.

Step 2: Prioritize

From the list that you have created above, circle three goals that you believe to be the most important to your success. Once you have identified three, transfer these goals to the lines below, ranking them in order of importance with 1 being the highest priority. Then, for each goal, assess the level of difficulty (1 = low; 10 = high) and intensity (1 = low; 10 = high) of the goal. By *difficulty,* we mean tough to manage or overcome. By *intensity,* we mean the severity of the emotion experienced. An example has been provided.

Example

1. *Changing the organization's climate*   Difficulty 9   Intensity 9

2. *Taking on more leadership responsibility*   Difficulty 5   Intensity 8

3. *Leading more group meetings*   Difficulty 3   Intensity 3

Your Goals

1. _____   Difficulty____   Intensity____

2. _____   Difficulty____   Intensity____

3. _____   Difficulty____   Intensity____

Step 3: Action Planning

For each of your three goals, complete the following action planning process. This process is the final step to ensuring your goals are effectively established, meaningful, and action oriented. In the space provided, rewrite your goal. Be sure that your goal adheres to the characteristics of effective goals (Specific, Measurable, Action Oriented, Realistic, and Timely). An example has been provided.

Example Goal

Changing the organization's culture

Why is this goal important to your success?

It is important to my success because I value my workplace. It has so much potential on an individual, group, and societal level.

What resources will you need to achieve your goal?

Many different human and organizational resources. I will need to get buy-in from upper management, human resources, and fellow employees. I will need a steering committee to take the project on. I will need to talk with the Finance department to get financial resources to fund the initiative.

What resources can you leverage to achieve your goal?

The executive team. Show them a business case or business cases of culture impacting morale and the organization's bottom line.

Take Action

Identify three actions/behaviors that you can accomplish on a regular basis that will help you achieve your goal stated above.

Action 1. *Do research on the area. See what impact organizational culture has on morale, retention, and individual and group performance.*

Action 2. *Examine to see if the initiative is feasible. Is it the right time? Do we have enough resources? Will others be interested in helping?*

Action 3. *Go to upper management with a detailed plan and presentation plan. There is a need to be prepared and confident.*

Signed: *John Doe*   Date: *June 20*

Witness: *Claudia Doe*   Date: *June 20*

Your Goal 1

Why is this goal important to your success?

What resources will you need to achieve your goal?

What resources can you leverage to achieve your goal?

Take Action

Identify three actions/behaviors that you can accomplish on a regular basis that will help you achieve your goal stated above.

Action 1.

Action 2.

Action 3.

Signed: _____ Date: _____

Witness: _____ Date: _____

Your Goal 2

Why is this goal important to your success?

What resources will you need to achieve your goal?

What resources can you leverage to achieve your goal?

Take Action

Identify three actions/behaviors that you can accomplish on a regular basis that will help you achieve your goal stated above.

Action 1.

Action 2.

Action 3.

Signed: _____ Date: _____

Witness: _____ Date: _____

Your Goal 3

Why is this goal important to your success?

What resources will you need to achieve your goal?

What resources can you leverage to achieve your goal?

Take Action

Identify three actions/behaviors that you can accomplish on a regular basis that will help you achieve your goal stated above.

Action 1.

Action 2.

Action 3.

Signed: _____ Date: _____

Witness: _____ Date: _____

Exercise

Daily Assessment and Reflection

Sustainable change requires motivation, awareness, and reinforcement. Unfortunately, our personal and professional environments are not always supportive of the change we desire, so we must take matters into our own hands.

Step 1: The Seven-Day Challenge

The use of daily observations and self-reinforcement is a highly effective method for implementing personal change. This activity is primarily self-directed and is designed to provide you with the steps necessary for change. If sustainable change is your goal, it will be your desire and attention to meticulous observation that are at the core of your success.

Make seven copies of the seven-day challenge log on the following pages. Each day, record the date and three challenges you faced. Answer the questions provided to explore the positive changes that can result from your efforts.

Today's Date:

Identify three challenges that you faced today and complete the questions for each one. Challenges may be large or small.

Challenge 1

What was your reaction to this challenge? (circle one)   Positive   Negative

How did you deal with this challenge? Record your thoughts and actions.

What was the outcome of your thoughts and action/inaction?

How could you have improved upon this situation (that is, thoughts and actions)?

What resources will you require (e.g., time, mentoring, coaching, human resources, physical resources, etc.)?

Challenge 2

What was your reaction to this challenge? (circle one)   Positive   Negative

How did you deal with this challenge? Record your thoughts and actions.

What was the outcome of your thoughts and action/inaction?

How could you have improved upon this situation (that is, thoughts and actions)?

What resources will you require (e.g., time, mentoring, coaching, human resources, physical resources, etc.)?

Challenge 3

What was your reaction to this challenge? (circle one)   Positive   Negative

How did you deal with this challenge? Record your thoughts and actions.

What was the outcome of your thoughts and action/inaction?

How could you have improved upon this situation (that is, thoughts and actions)?

What resources will you require (e.g., time, mentoring, coaching, human resources, physical resources, etc.)?

Step 2: Change the Way You See the Problem

Use the table below to record your key thoughts and actions. If your thoughts/actions are negative, rewrite them in a positive tone that allows you to move forward with a solution to the problem.

Now take a minute to replay your thoughts/actions in your mind as you see yourself successfully surmounting your challenges. If you managed to remain positive in the face of a challenge, fantastic! Record how you faced the challenge and be sure to replay your success in your mind to reinforce your positive actions. Positive thinking and action planning will help increase your tendency for using these strategies in future encounters!

		Key Thoughts/Actions	Positive Alternative
Day 1	Challenge 1		
	Challenge 2		
	Challenge 3		

Emotional Intelligence Skills Assessment (EISA)

		Key Thoughts/Actions	Positive Alternative
Day 2	Challenge 1		
	Challenge 2		
	Challenge 3		
Day 3	Challenge 1		
	Challenge 2		
	Challenge 3		
Day 4	Challenge 1		
	Challenge 2		
	Challenge 3		

		Key Thoughts/Actions	Positive Alternative
Day 5	Challenge 1		
	Challenge 2		
	Challenge 3		
Day 6	Challenge 1		
	Challenge 2		
	Challenge 3		
Day 7	Challenge 1		
	Challenge 2		
	Challenge 3		

Emotional Intelligence Skills Assessment (EISA)

Influencing

Exercise

Influencing Log

In order to develop your EISA skills, they must be practiced and honed each and every day. The daily Influencing Log is designed to provide a self-analysis of your ability to effectively perceive and manage your emotions. More importantly, this activity will help you identify how your emotions affect both your thoughts and actions and your ability to apply your emotional intelligence for positive influence in others. A sample is provided on this page; the following page is a blank form for your use.

Step 1: Events and Interactions

Describe a key social event that occurred for you today.

Introduced a new project to a newly created cross-functional team

Step 2: Influence

Describe a situation that occurred today in which you were able to respond to or inspire the emotions of others in order to influence their thoughts and actions.

Discussed the importance of the project to the overall goals of the organization, discussed why this team was assembled for this specific project, discussed the strengths of the group, and project timelines

Step 3: Application

Describe how you applied your knowledge of emotions to influence the judgments, decision making, and actions of those you interact with.

Spoke with enthusiasm about the project to evoke emotions and feelings in group members

Step 4: Appraise

How effective was your attempt to apply your emotional intelligence for influencing the emotions, thoughts, and actions of others? What could you have done differently to increase your social awareness?

Use more powerful emotional and social words (e.g., we, us, optimism, overcoming challenges together, etc.), make more eye contact with the group, show a bit more confidence

---

Emotional Intelligence Skills Assessment (EISA)

Influencing Log

Step 1: Events and Interactions

Describe a key social event that occurred for you today.

Step 2: Influence

Describe a situation that occurred today in which you were able to respond to or inspire the emotions of others in order to influence their thoughts and actions.

Step 3: Application

Describe how you applied your knowledge of emotions to influence the judgments, decision making, and actions of those you interact with.

Step 4: Appraise

How effective was your attempt to apply your emotional intelligence for influencing the emotions, thoughts, and actions of others? What could you have done differently to increase your social awareness?

Exercise

Modeling

The ability to regulate and evoke particular emotions can directly impact the quality and intensity of a social relationship. Your emotional expressiveness can color your message, influencing the way people read and react to you, the values that you uphold, and the amount of power, competence, and credibility that you maintain. Remaining confident and authentic in your interactions with people is also an essential component to becoming more influential in the various roles that you play. Being able to express yourself clearly and confidently often motivates others to achieve higher levels of performance.

The objective of this exercise is to enhance your ability to deliver your message in a meaningful and inspirational manner.

Step 1: Identify Great Leaders

The first step in this process is to identify three great leaders. Spend time searching for examples of speeches they have delivered and interviews they have given.

Leader 1

What makes this person a great leader?

Describe how this person used emotional cues and content to convey his or her message.

Briefly, restate the message of this speech or interview.

Was the message conveyed effectively? Why or why not?

Describe the body language and facial expressions used by this individual.

Leader 2

What makes this person a great leader?

Describe how this person used emotional cues and content to convey his or her message.

Briefly, restate the message of this speech or interview.

Was the message conveyed effectively? Why or why not?

Describe the body language and facial expressions used by this individual.

Leader 3

What makes this person a great leader?

Describe how this person used emotional cues and content to convey his or her message.

Briefly, restate the message of this speech or interview.

Was the message conveyed effectively? Why or why not?

Describe the body language and facial expressions used by this individual.

Step 2: Summarize and Analyze

Now that you have identified three great leaders, all of whom have unique strengths and limitations, it is important for you to compare them with each other and compare yourself with them.

What characteristics do these leaders have in common?

What do they do differently?

How do you compare? Be specific!

In order for you to convey your message more effectively, what three changes could you make in the future?

1.

2.

3.

Group Challenges Exercise

The objective of this exercise is to further your understanding of how emotions can be influential in a social setting.

In this exercise you will write down the three greatest group challenges that you are currently facing. For each challenge, place a check mark under the emotional intelligence skills that you believe you need to use more frequently in order to have more influence over this challenge. For each skill that you choose, indicate how the greater use of this skill will be beneficial to you and to the group that you are working with.

Step 1: Record the Challenges

Record the three greatest group challenges you are currently facing. For each group challenge put a check mark in the EISA skills box that you believe you would like to leverage more often in order to achieve greater social influence. A sample has been provided.

Group Challenges	Perceiving	Managing	Decision Making	Achieving	Influencing
Motivating direct reports	✓	✓		✓	

In order for me to motivate my direct reports to achieve their goals, I must:

1. Perceive their emotions on a daily basis in order to understand how they are feeling as well as to understand what emotions are needed to motivate each person, since each person is different.

2. Manage my own emotions and the emotions of others, especially close to deadlines. Try to understand what are the stressors involved in obtaining goals and, once there is an understanding, come up with various coping mechanisms.

3. Understand which reports are working hard to achieve their goals and which ones are having difficulty. Treat each direct report differently. Each has his or her own unique challenges.

Group Challenges	Perceiving	Managing	Decision Making	Achieving	Influencing

Step 2: Describe the Benefit
Group Challenge 1

My goal is to increase the use of the following emotional intelligence skills:

If I use more of these skills, I will realize the following individual and group benefits:

Group Challenge 2

My goal is to increase the use of the following emotional intelligence skills:

If I use more of these skills, I will realize the following individual and group benefits:

Group Challenge 3

My goal is to increase the use of the following emotional intelligence skills:

If I use more of these skills, I will realize the following individual and group benefits:

Development Strategies

Perceiving

- Make a point of watching other people's emotional reactions during interactions. Also listen to words others use that may have emotional content to them. This will allow you to perceive and understand other people's emotional information more accurately.

- Genuinely listen to others without any distractions. Listen to the emotional content in the words they use and try not to superimpose your values and beliefs on what the person is saying. This will allow you to remain unbiased and present in the conversation.

- When listening to others, also pay close attention to nonverbal cues like facial expressions and body posture. For facial expressions, emotional changes are evident in someone's forehead, eyebrows, mouth, and wrinkles around the eyes. This added information will allow you to perceive and understand other people's emotional information more accurately.

- In order to improve your active listening skills, practice paraphrasing what others are saying to you. Do not simply repeat what was said; use different words that express the same meaning. This will make people feel that you are actively engaged in the conversation.

- If you used an EISA: 360, look at which group is rating you much lower than you rated yourself. Ask members of the group for specific examples of when you did not use this ability effectively.

Managing

- How do you respond to stressful situations? Research has shown that in stressful situations your body responds to your emotions before your mind does. Ask yourself, what message is my body sending me? For example, when stressed, do you experience increased shoulder tension? When anxious, do you experience more gastrointestinal symptoms? Make a note of any physical reactions that you've had at the time or shortly after feeling stressed. Pay attention to what makes these sensations more or less intense.

- Are you able to manage your emotions effectively during conflict? In order to deal with conflict effectively, you must be aware of stimuli that result in negative emotional reactions. If negative emotions do occur, what skills do you have at your disposal to put you in the right frame of mind to tackle the issue at hand?

- Conduct a self-inventory on controlling your emotions. Have there been times when you have made rash decisions because you were overwhelmed by emotions or were biased by them? If so, look to see whether there are any patterns to when you have made impulsive decisions.

- Remember times at which your work performance has suffered while you felt overwhelmed. Try to understand how the feeling of being stressed has affected your planning, problem solving, and interpersonal relationships.

- Explore how often your self-talk accompanies your managing emotions skills. For example, have your negative feelings toward a co-worker influenced how you interacted with this person? Understand how your emotions and feelings toward certain situations or individuals bias your judgment in regard to decision making and relationships.

- Whenever you are in a position to act impulsively—Stop, Take a Deep Breath, and Think. This will give you extra time to think about alternative actions.

- If you used an EISA: 360, look at which group is rating you much lower than you rated yourself. Ask members of the group for specific examples of when you did not fully use this ability effectively.

Decision Making

- Ask yourself, what impact do emotions have on my decision making? For example, do you have a tendency to make decisions impulsively under stress? When making decisions, try to understand whether emotions are biasing your decision-making process. If so, incorporate some of the strategies from the Perceiving and Managing factors. These strategies will help you to recognize and regulate the emotions necessary to get you in the right frame of mind to decide effectively.

- Knowing which emotions will help you resolve a problem is critical to your success. When creativity is in order, recognize which positive emotions most facilitate generating ideas and seeing possibilities.

- Conducting a SWOT analysis may help to guide you in making more effective decisions. Being able to identify a situation's strengths, weaknesses, opportunities, and threats will help to identify internal and external supports (strengths and opportunities) as well as internal and external challenges (weaknesses and threats). Please keep aware of emotional biases or positive/negative reactions when identifying specific areas of the SWOT analysis.

- Before arriving at a decision or determination of a course of action, generate multiple alternatives with pros and cons for each to ensure that you are addressing the unique attributes of the problem. Make a conscious effort to assimilate new information as needed.

- Ask questions to accurately identify the problem. Instead of following implicit assumptions, gather facts that can serve as the basis for constructing a relevant solution. Furthermore, define the scope of the problem according to whether it affects an individual, team, or the entire corporation.

- Whenever possible, use a multi-step strategy when making decisions: proposed solution, verification of solutions (such as pilot testing, second opinions) and, only then, implementation. Formal documentation of the pros and cons of alternative actions will also help you to avoid rash decisions.

- If you used an EISA: 360, look at which group is rating you much lower than you rated yourself. Ask members of the group for specific examples of when you did not fully use this ability effectively.

Achieving

- Engage in self-exploration exercises with your raters (especially your manager). Write down a list of your strengths, and ask your raters to write lists of your strengths as well. Once you have pinpointed your areas of strength, create an action plan with your raters to incorporate a plan to fully leverage these skills in various situations. Make sure to use this skill consistently, not just with a certain group or in a particular setting.

- Increase your level of achievement by recognizing the successful efforts of your team and your own individual accomplishments. Record at least one event per day. Make sure these efforts are celebrated.

- Determine your short-term, intermediate, and long-term goals, both your own and your work group's. Think about your skill set, both strengths and development areas, and how they relate to your goals. Finally, formulate an action plan to address any gaps in your skill set that may impact goal achievement.

- With the help of your manager, set individual and team goals that are challenging yet obtainable. Remember to create goals that are specific, measurable, and action oriented.

- Articulate your course of action. An action plan specifically outlines activities that need to be done at various points in time in order to successfully implement your recommendation.

- Once you have a clear idea of the direction in which you want to head, be sure to monitor your progress of achieving those self-development goals over time. This will reduce the possibility of procrastination. If there is procrastination during the goal achievement process, try to understand what emotions are leading to this hesitation on your part.

- If you used an EISA: 360, look at which group is rating you much lower than you rated yourself. Ask members of the group for specific examples of when you did not fully use this ability effectively.

Influencing

- Consider asking your raters how you come across when interacting during individual and group encounters. Ask them whether you show a different level of confidence and assertiveness with different groups. If this is the case, formulate a plan for these different encounters that will allow you to best impart your ideas.

- When working on your influencing skills, be conscious of your body language, tone of voice, and timing when delivering your message. These components may add to or take away from the message you are trying to convey.

- Smile. Yes, it is just that simple. You will appear more approachable and will make a lasting impression on others.

- If you are having difficulty having influence with certain rater groups, find someone who is qualified to mentor you. Talk to this person about his or her leadership experiences and observe him or her in leadership situations. This will allow you to learn new strategies and techniques that will allow you to share your ideas with others.

- If you are lacking influence in certain situations, try visualizing yourself performing the skill to perfection. Picture yourself feeling confident and successfully asserting your opinions without being overpowering, while at the same time enjoying the moment of the interaction.

- If you used an EISA: 360, look at which group is rating you much lower than you rated yourself. Ask members of that group for specific examples of when you did not use this ability effectively.

Resources
and Endnotes

Books

EQ Edge by Steve Stein and Howard Book

Emotional Intelligence in Action by Marcia Hughes, L. Bonita Patterson, and James Terrell

The Emotionally Intelligent Manager by David Caruso and Peter Salovey

EQ Leader Program by Dana Ackley, Multi-Health Systems Inc.

The Handbook of Emotional Intelligence by Reuven Bar-On and James Parker

Emotional Intelligence by Daniel Goleman

Working with Emotional Intelligence by Daniel Goleman

Descartes' Error: Emotion, Reason and the Human Brain by Antonio Damasio

Emotions and Life: Perspectives from Psychology, Biology, and Evolution by Robert Plutchik

Handbook for Developing Emotional and Social Intelligence by Marcia Hughes, James Terrell, and H.D. Thompson.

Websites

Pfeiffer website http://www.pfeiffer.com

MHS' Emotional Intelligence and Human Capital website: http://www.mhs.com/eihc.aspx

Consortium for Research on Emotional Intelligence in Organizations: http://www.eiconsortium.org/

Micro Expression Training Tool: http://www.mettonline.com/

Human Capital Institute Emotional Intelligence and Human Capital: http://www.humancapitalinstitute.org/hci/tracks_emotional_intelligence.guid

Endnotes

1. Sue-Chan, C., & Latham, G.P. (2004). The situational interview as a predictor of academic and team performance: A study of the mediating effects of cognitive ability and emotional intelligence. *International Journal of Selection and Assessment, 12*, 312–320.

2. Bachman, J., Stein, S.J., Campbell, K., & Sitarenios, G. (2000). Emotional intelligence in the collection of debt. *International Journal of Selection and Assessment, 8,* 176–182.

3. George, J.M. (2000). Emotions and leadership: The role of emotional intelligence. *Human Relations, 53*, 1027–1055.

   Rubin, R.S., Munz, D.C., & Bommer, W.H. (2005). Leading from within: The effects of emotion recognition and personality on transformational leadership behavior. *Academy of Management Journal, 48*, 845–858.

4. Mann, D., & Papadogiannis, P. (2008). *EISA research and technical report*. San Francisco: Pfeiffer.

5. Jacobsen, E. (1938). *Progressive relaxation*. Chicago: University of Chicago Press.

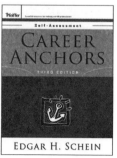